T0207977

FOCUS ON "ME" BEFORE "I" BECOMES "WE!"

EIGHT STEPS TO BECOMING A BETTER YOU (BEFORE, WHILE, OR AFTER A RELATIONSHIP/MARRIAGE)

MiMi831

BALBOA.PRESS

A DIVISION OF HAY HOUSE

Balboa Press books may be ordered through booksellers or by contacting:

Balboa Press
A Division of Hay House
1663 Liberty Drive
Bloomington, IN 47403
www.balboapress.com
1 (877) 407-4847

Print information available on the last page.

ISBN: 978-1-9822-3978-7 (sc)
ISBN: 978-1-9822-3979-4 (e)

Balboa Press rev. date: 12/09/2019

CONTENTS

ACKNOWLEDGMENTS

First and foremost, I am thankful to God for allowing me this opportunity to use my life as a path for someone else as they learn for themselves how to transition through their life. It's my prayer that this book will assist, transform, and provide healing for the lost, broken, or weary.

I would like to dedicate this book to my angel. In spite of my approach to motherhood at a young age, regardless of what or where I took her in this life, her precious smile and genuine personality has never tarnished. I love you, baby!

To my parents, words cannot express my level of gratitude for the love and consistency you have shown me throughout these trying years of my life. It hasn't always been peachy, but the difficult times have really drawn us closer. I love you guys.

To my row dawgs, ace boon coons, my vanilla and caramel drops, my siblings, each of you has stretched me in a different way, even when I didn't want it to be. Overall it helped mold me into the woman I am today, and I am forever grateful to you all. My family is my rock, glue, and safe place. With God and my family, I know the sky is the limit.

Last but not least, to my grandmother. You have been such a great inspiration to many. You are missed and loved dearly. REST IN HEAVEN MIMI. 8-letters, 3-words, 1-meaning. I LOVE YOU!

INTRODUCTION

It came to me many times in a dream that one of the reasons I was placed on this earth was to endure some unthinkable things throughout life. These things would mold me into a strong individual yet allow me the ability to use my experiences to help others. There was no other better way of me beginning to do that, other than using the tools and methods I had to use myself so I could find my way through some of my hardest times in my life.

So that is how this self-help workbook came about. I wanted to help other people who may experience life as I have as well as encourage, empower, and assist them in any and every area of their lives. As I will share more in detail throughout the book, when things started to become very dark, low, and unbearable for me personally, I had to take certain measures to make sure my mental or emotional state didn't affect me. Now I am living life to the fullest, and when I smile, it is actually sincere. So that is what this book is for, to help you break down your mess and rebuild you.

I hope you realize the statement I made. I said *rebuild* and not just *build*. Let me say it like this: you can build on a broken, cracked, or damaged foundation; however, at some point, those cracks and damages will begin to reveal in your foundation. This same concept applies to you as a person; your outer appearance may look great and well put together. But your makeup (your interior) is slowly but surely falling apart. At some point, the interior will begin to affect the exterior.

Some areas in this book will require you to break your situation all the way down or face areas that you are just not ready to. However, in order to become a better you, you have to acknowledge what you are pretending doesn't exist. That was one of my toughest challenges, facing what I felt I refused to face or believe about myself. But when I actually did it—I mean for real did it—I have to tell you that I felt so much lighter (burden-wise). I slept with so much peace knowing that I took those necessary measures to face the unbearable times in my life.

During the rebuild process for me, God gave the idea of a self-help book to my mind. Experience is one of the best tools of learning; therefore, if I came out on top of my situation, there is nothing more important to me in this world than to be able to help you come out of your situation better, stronger, and wiser than when you went in.

Everyone talks about the importance of being married, setting down, and living right, but nobody highlights the importance of singleness, self-worth, and self-development in order to have a productive and prosperous marriage. This is some of the hard work some may face before encountering marriage. Others may experience while they are married or even have had a failed marriage. This is a process that anyone can take, regardless of where you are in life.

I encourage you to say a prayer before beginning this journey and really asking God to relieve every dark area and emotion necessary to render complete healing from every encounter of your life. And ask him to give you the strength to face the good, bad, and ugly so true healing can take place while you complete this process. If you are sincere with yourself, your work, and this process, I know without a doubt you will benefit in many areas. If you complete the process, you will also experience growth for yourself and your future.

Trust your process. That is what we will focus on, you building who you are and becoming the best you possible. This must occur before you are able to give any part of yourself to anyone. Trust me. During the time of my transition, I was hurt and blindsided. I didn't understand any of it, but now looking back from where I came from, I constantly thank God for bringing me out on top. Through my process, I have realized how strong of a woman I really am and how much my faith in God has grown. To be very transparent with you, I had no idea I had this much faith. Most times you don't realize it until it's tested.

It is my desire that you use this book to begin healing yourself and allowing God to start the transformation of who you are and who you are meant to be. During this time, don't think about Mr. Right. Don't ponder when you are going to get married. And so forth and so on.

Release your mind from the stress of tomorrow. Live today for today, and live it to its fullest. Every day, really try to focus on being happy, positive, and peaceful as well as living in the moment. If you really focus on that throughout this book, I guarantee you will see a difference in yourself at the end of your process.

This book is for every season: single, dating, engaged, married, and divorced.

MY STORY

I became a mother at a young age (most would say). I was pregnant at twenty-one. More importantly, I wasn't married. When I found out I was pregnant, I was devastated because I had never wanted kids and never wanted to be a baby mama. I had always been mature for my age, but not enough to be raising a child by myself.

I tried my hardest to make things work with my daughter's father, but it just wasn't going to happen. There was too much hurt, along with lots of areas where I felt he should have been involved. I had to make the decision to move on from the relationship and focus solely on me.

When I say me, I mean I didn't want to have a child. I didn't have the time to raise one alone. I was about three and a half months pregnant when I went to the abortion clinic. I knew this was something I had to do. I remember this day precisely. I walked into this clinic and saw many girls with their mothers or their partners, preparing to end a life. Here I was about to do the same thing. From the moment I had gotten into the car to the time I got on the table, I had terrible stomach pain. Yet I signed in, paid the fee, and waited patiently.

My time in the lobby seemed to bring up everything in my life. I felt numb to everything. Time seemed to be taking so long before finally I was called to the back area.

I lay on the table as they mounted my legs to begin the procedure, thinking this was not the life I had envisioned for myself. Tears ran down my face. Just the thought of killing this living creature, a part of me, was taking a toll on me.

Then I lay there alone, trying to prepare myself for this, for three minutes, which felt like three hours. All I thought was, *There is no way I will be able to take care of a child*. And that moment was the very first time I heard God speak to me. He was as clear as day, like someone sitting in front of me.

He asked, "Do you trust me?" Then he said what was in the Bible. "I will never leave you nor forsake you" (Deuteronomy 31:6).

I began to question what I was hearing. I asked, "God, is this really you? Assure me this is you."

I knew of many who had heard the voice of God because I swear my grandmother was like God's best friend. They had many conversations! But I had yet to experience him for myself.

Once I got quiet and set at the clinic, I realized it was taking the nurse so long to come back for a reason. I noticed my stomach wasn't hurting anymore. The tears had stopped flowing from my face. A level of assurance and peace flooded over my full body. At that moment, I recognized that I could not do this. I would have to endure the pregnancy and motherhood, whether I was alone or not. So now I am a mother to a little girl. I have taken great pride in learning to raise this jewel.

The next choice I had to make was not easy, but I had to choose him or me. After some time, I decided to end the relationship with my daughter's father. I chose to solely focus on my child and me. I had to make sure I was the best mother I could be, which meant I had to limit any and all distractions that could cause me to lose my focus.

Unnecessary heartaches and pain meant nothing at this point. Even though we would no longer be together, I very much wanted my daughter's father to be present in her life. Honestly, I didn't make every experience as easy as possible for him, but that was because I was still dealing with past hurt.

I was single for three years before even entertaining the thought of dating. I decided to never bring any of my male friends, dates, or boyfriends around my daughter. I didn't see the need for her to meet everyone I met. I didn't enter a committed relationship for about four years, when I met my now ex-husband.

Before that, I made sure I aligned myself as a mother first. Making sure I was content within myself and wasn't spending unnecessary time away from her was important before I gave up any part of me to dating.

Our relationship did not start out fast. We were friends for about two years before we officially entered a relationship. Occasionally, we were friends with benefits, but there was genuine friendship that was built (so I thought). We had beautiful families and friends and were surrounded by people who truly wanted the best for us (or at least for him). After having a friendship of two years and dating for three years, we finally got engaged and married. But let me go into a little more detail for you.

After two years of dating, he met my family. We did a lot of things together. We never lived together, but we had the family dynamic going on. We did things altogether. I took care of him and did for him like I was already his wife. (That's where I messed up). So naturally I was trying to figure out why he was not asking me to marry him. I wondered, *Why is he taking so long?*

On my birthday, I went out to dinner with his family. He came and got my daughter, and he said he needed her help with something. I was getting all excited because I was thinking he was preparing to propose to me. But that night came to an end … and nothing.

I was so devastated that evening that I ended things with him. I felt like I had to make it clear that he had become too comfortable in the relationship and he would have to leave me alone if he didn't have a desire to marry me.

We were broken up for a few days, and then I began feeling how many women do. I thought, *Well, maybe I rushed him,* and *I don't want to start all over.* So of course I went to him to fix things, and we ended up back together. I decided to just leave the whole marriage thing alone.

Sure enough, about five months later, he unexpectedly proposed to me. The proposal was great; I was totally surprised. The part that caught me off guard on this perfect surprise was when he said, "Only thing is you can't tell anyone yet because I haven't been able to get your father on the phone to ask for his blessings."

I was shocked. This man was fully aware of the type of relationship my father and I had, with so many mixed feelings and the desire to be married. I just went along with it. Yeah! I know it's a red flag.

It seemed like everything happened so fast after getting engaged. There were a lot of red flags, but when you are in love, you don't pay attention to them as you should. I made clear to him that I wanted to move back to Texas, where my family was. He made clear he wanted to go as well. I made clear that I was not about to shack up with him, simply because I had a child. There were no exceptions.

Then the talk came about getting married now and having a wedding later. So that's what we did. All his relatives were at the wedding; none of mine were. Things went too fast. Before I knew it, we were married and on the road to Texas, heading back into my normal world, which he was not ready to participate in.

Sure enough, six months into our marriage, there was infidelity. I was always that chick who said, "If you cheat on me, I'm done." And that's where I was this time. But I stayed in my marriage. I honored my vows too much to give up just yet. With much prayer, counseling, and time spent together, it seemed that we were just going through the motions.

One year and three months later, I found myself questioning whether I should leave the marriage. My desires to fix the union failed, along with counseling sessions, disbelief, pastoral concern, infidelity, disrespect, and betrayal. Five months later, I found myself filing for divorce.

At first, I wanted to stay in the marriage to avoid embarrassment or feelings of shame and failure, but a marriage takes two people who mutually love, respect, and honor the union. I had heard many people say how they fought for their marriage or how their spouse changed, and here I was carrying this load all alone. I realized I was fighting for something that was not working. After being hurt, unhappy, and mistreated for so long, I got tired.

While still married, I began to experience terrible stomach pains. I later found out I had to get my gallbladder removed. Only weeks later I found out I needed surgery on both wrists due to a terrible case of carpal tunnel syndrome.

My husband and I agreed that I would leave work to handle these issues because I was in terrible pain.

Leaving work meant my main source of income would change; however, I made sure I kept money coming in so the bulk of the load was not put on my husband. My marriage began to go through a hardship. It became obvious that we were just going through the motions. Like most women, I felt I couldn't leave my situation because I didn't have a job. I would occasionally help my mother with her business when I was physically able to, but I still didn't have a steady income.

Daily I prayed, asking God to fix my marriage or show me the way to walk away. I eventually made the decision to separate. And after two weeks of being separated, I tell you God literally laid things out for me. This is just what he did. I didn't have a full-time job, I was still in school full time, and I had the responsibility of financially taking care of my daughter.

To sum it all up for you, we broke the lease on the apartment we had. I had to pay half the money to break that contract. Yet I had the money for that. Then God made a way for me to get a house for my daughter and me. All of this happened while I was making sure my daughter stayed on A honor roll and I was testing out of classes so I could graduate five months early. God provided everything I asked for, and through it all, my finances never hit hardship throughout the whole process. I didn't worry for the first time in life. I just knew it had to be done. I prayed, and it was done. You can't tell me that I don't serve a great God!

I wished no ill will toward my ex-husband at the time, but I wanted nothing else to do with the marriage or the possibility of affecting my child's mental and emotional state from witnessing this harsh treatment. When I love, I love extremely hard, and I give so much. But this is one situation where I'd given all I could. I compromised my self-worth to inflate someone else's pride and ego. It was only best for me to walk away before I had resentment toward him or myself for staying in something that wasn't changing. To this day, I have a sincere love for him and his family, and I wish nothing but pure happiness for him in life, but as for me, this whole chapter has ended.

Now realize that I wasn't in love with him; I was in love with his family and the dynamic in which they functioned because that was what I needed from my family. The funny thing is, as God isolated me from everything I had known when moving to another state, he was also working on my behalf.

I left home with so much heart as well as divided relationships and family. My parents were divorced after a twenty-one-year marriage. It all had fallen apart so fast, but then I returned home to my family, now healed, restored, and standing there with open arms. My parents had healed their relationship and found love in each other again. Now I was able to give and receive anything and everything within the dynamics of my own family.

In transitioning my life, I realized that it was not just about me. I had to put my feelings aside. I had to make sure that my daughter was mentally and emotionally okay. She had become very close to him as well as his family, and she had an extremely close bond with his aunt. I then realized that no one will ever love your child like you do. Nonetheless, I remember what his Word says, "I will never leave you nor forsake you" (Deuteronomy 31:6).

What is crazy is my daughter began to mentally transition before I even decided to leave my husband. You know how kids can sense things? When I sat down and explained the changes to her, she understood, and the whole process was so smooth with her. In everything we did, I made sure I covered my marriage, my child, and our life in prayer, so I knew it was nothing but God who carried my child and me through this transition.

Let me be clear. I'm not saying that God is one for divorce, but when man or brokenness brings you together, it's not God. At that point, God has no doing. The confusion comes when you try to get God to work a miracle on something you created yourself. This part is very confusing to me.

So many people say that divorce is not the answer and the marriage will be turned around if you put it in God's hand. I am a true believer of that; however, I was in a marriage where the intentions were all wrong on both sides. He wanted someone to help him escape the life he was stuck in, and I wanted my happily ever after right now. I wanted my marriage to be one of ministry, to not only help us individually and as a couple, but to also be a help to others due to our unique situations. I spent many nights on my face crying out to God because I wanted him to turn around what I put together. Yet I failed to remember that there were lies, deceit, and infidelity while we were dating. So why on earth would I think marriage would force a person to change and grow up?

I am saying that to assert this: pay attention to those red flags when they come. Marriage can be hard and requires a lot of work. However, none of that matters if you don't start with a level of respect for yourself and one another. For me personally, that's where I had a hard time. I had found security and protection in this man. Then I had to later realize that he was able to protect me from everyone else, but not the hurt he was causing me. It was necessary for me to get out of that marriage if I wanted to have an ounce of confidence, love, or value for myself.

So now I was going into my thirties as a single mother and a soon-to-be divorcée. That sounds so crazy to me! But when I tell you my level of faith has grown tremendously throughout this separation and divorce and I have seen how strong of a woman I am, I am blown away by this whole experience. I don't have one negative impression toward marriage, dating, or even love. Let me tell you. My faith went to an all-time high!

When it comes to my purpose, I know one is supposed to be a wife. I just tried to rush things. That's where I went wrong. Nevertheless, the experience of this first marriage has built me so much and prepared me for my next union.

My daughter's father made the decision not to be in her life because of feelings he had toward our relationship ending many years ago. For seven years, he missed out—no phone calls, birthdays, Christmas, or anything! I tell you everything happens for a reason.

Two weeks after I decided to leave my husband, her father began to reach out and contact my daughter. He was making arrangements and actually following through with those plans in seeing her, consistently calling her, and so on. I saw a smile on my daughter's face that I had never seen. A relationship was forming for her that my ex-husband had made clear he never wanted to happen.

So I found it crazy how things had happened because we had no contact with her father for years (by his choosing). This was a relationship that I had decided to step out of the way and allow to flourish on its own. I could tell that my daughter was looking for her father's love. She wanted him to be present in her life. It seemed as everything was happening at the same time I was wrapping up a marriage while my daughter was exploring a new relationship with her father, something she had always wanted. Regardless of what I was going through, I knew I had to put it aside and actually be there for my daughter as she embarked on this brand-new experience.

As women, we tend to harp on ill will toward the father for not being there and the past hurts they put us through. Instead we refuse to forgive and move on, which ultimately affects the child more than you because you are not allowing them to harvest the full benefits of having both parents in their lives. When I learned for myself that I was hurting my daughter by holding these ill feelings toward her father, I decided that to end so my daughter would get all she needed from both her father and me.

The power of forgiveness is so strong! I forgave my daughter's father a couple of years ago, but you really don't know if that forgiveness is real until you are face-to-face with the person. The first time I witnessed my daughter's father with her after he reached out, I felt sincere love for the forming relationship. I then realized that true forgiveness is not just for the other person. It's for me! Because I forgave him, I was able to assist both of them in certain areas to help rebuild their relationship.

That process allowed me to further my ability of forgiveness. Little did I know, while I was helping my daughter, I was assisting myself. I began to forgive myself for the failed marriage I just endured. In doing so, I was able to move forward with the divorce without the desire to look back or put any energy in getting even. I had a sincere desire to move forward with my life in pure happiness, peace, and love.

What's the mind-blowing part? This is something I gained from my daughter. After all the years her father missed in her life, she still had that calming spirit of love and peace as well as the desire to be happy. That brought a ray of sunlight in my life when I thought it was the darkest time. This seven-year-old taught me something!

This time of life was vital for me. I had to learn how to move forward. I am grateful that this was a learning experience that I actually defeated and I didn't allow to defeat me. This little girl I was about to abort, God had better plans in store for her life as well as mine. Lord knows where I would be right now if I didn't have this little girl next to me.

As I patiently waited for my divorce to be finalized, I focused on school, graduating five months early and strengthening my relationship with God, family, and my daughter. As you can see, my story may not sound perfect to you, but it is to me because it's my story. My story may not be your story, but you have one as well. This shaped me into the women I am today and helped me get to the point of living a happy and peaceful life.

We make decisions in life that we expect to turn out perfect, but we find ourselves angry, sad, and hurt because things don't turn out the way we planned them to. You have to understand. For every tear you've cried, there is a rainbow ahead. Your struggle will bring you true happiness. If you never go through anything, how do expect to be happy and secure in where you are now? We all have to learn to embrace who we are and what we are going through.

My fears have made me stronger, my tears have made me wiser, and my dedication has made me successful. I no longer fear raising my daughter in a single-parent household. I no longer question my role as a mother, some of the detours I made in life, or my ability to be the best in everything I do. I am a strong, beautiful, educated black woman who loves life as she faces the future and accepts the different milestones in her life.

Now let's focus on your story. That is what this book emphasizes, you building who you are and becoming the best you possible before you are able to become one with anyone. The importance of knowing your story, as everyone has one, is what makes you *you*. Everybody has a totally different story, and yours is unique to you. It is the molding of your foundation in life.

I have opened up and shared my story because I wanted you to realize how vital specific details are to facing your truth and living out your reality. I also wanted you to understand how being honest with yourself about the dark and embarrassing moments will help you heal completely. I have learned to accept and embrace my story. That is why I am able to share it openly and identify areas where I know I needed healing and growth.

When answering the questions below, take the time to really think and be honest with yourself. No one else is reading this, but you should really dig deep in completing your story. Once you write it down, take the time and read it over and over until you understand and embrace your story! Remember, it is your story. It was your story then, it will be your story today, and it will be your story tomorrow!

You will never understand your purpose until you understand your story.

Questions

1. Have you written your story? If not, what is stopping you?

_____

_____

_____

_____

_____

2. What is your story?

_____

_____

_____

_____

_____

_____

_____

_____

_____

_____

_____

_____

_____

_____

_____

Let's begin the steps!

STEP 1

FINDING AND UNDERSTANDING YOU!

Each one of us is born with a purpose of some type. Many of us have yet to find or understand what that purpose entails. However, you will never understand your purpose in life until you know and understand who you are. Who you are and your purpose are two things that are different yet work together to fulfill one another. If you hesitate about whom you are, then you will begin to question your purpose as well. I will go into further detail on the importance of you understanding and fulfilling your purpose later in this process. Right now, I want to focus on finding yourself and understanding who you are.

Finding yourself means taking the time to understand who you are at your very core, what you are about, and what you stand for. Several people go back and look at their historical roots to begin to understand themselves. That's fine; however, where you come from doesn't always have to define who you are. In most aspects, that will only happen if you allow it. Your historical makeup will only add gestures to the qualities you already possess.

Oftentimes I found myself hurt, brokenhearted, thirsty for love, and roaming in all the wrong areas. Then I started to question what was wrong with me and then compared myself to other people. It wasn't until I literally hit rock bottom or no one answered my calls or called me. At that point, I realized that no one would ever have the answers I needed because the answers were trapped within me.

Regardless of what I did or how hard someone else tried, I would never have happiness because I wasn't happy. True happiness comes from within; you have to find happiness through yourself before someone else ever will. For some reason, I couldn't wrap my mind around why I wasn't able to make myself happy. So in 2010, I decided to seek help, choosing to see a counselor to better dive into the situation. I was about three sessions in, as normal topics and questions would come up. Everything was moving along, that is, until the counselor asked me, "Who are you?"

I have never been so speechless in my life. I've always had the ability to think quickly and have an instant comeback, but in this time and moment, I was lost for words. Not having the answer to that question left me with a real embarrassed feeling because in truth I really didn't know the answer to that. At that moment, I realized that because I didn't know who I was, there was only so much I could recognize or share about myself. There would always be a surface understanding of details about the real me.

When you don't know who you are and what you stand for, that will cause you to fall for anything and everything. When you know who you are, you can build yourself up to a level of confidence from within. You can begin to set and build morals and values you will want to live by because those are standards you don't compromise. My problem was that I had no core understanding of who I was and what I stood for, so all I knew is what others believed or said about me to be true.

I found myself so embarrassed by that question that I didn't have the guts to return for more counseling. From that day, many sleepless nights came, along with a bunch of confusion that I determined would put out an all-out search for who I was. I had to answer that question for myself.

I began the process of trying to better understand my family, as if they were who I was, or judging my own past to provide a guide in the direction as to who I was. The answer came thirteen days later. I decided to do the work to figure out who I was. I was a young single mother. I wanted to better myself before I destroyed any chance of my daughter having her mother become a role model, a woman of standards and purpose, the things I should already stand as. I decided to bring another human into this world, to risk raising her. Even though I was lost, broken, and hurt, I knew I needed to fix this.

My process began with me taking at least thirty minutes each morning to meditate. During my transition, I lived at home with my parents. I would sit on the bathroom floor with my back leaned up against the bathtub and my legs stretched out in front of me, meditating. Using those thirty minutes to breathe, release, and prepare made all of the difference for my day. I have always been a worrywart, so me using each morning to meditate really helps me to release a lot of things I tend to think or ponder over. Then I realized I had become what people thought of me. Then I could actually speak into my own life and believe the things I was speaking about myself.

If you think negative thoughts, then you begin to speak negative talk. So I placed colored sticky notes behind my bed, so that each morning when I rose out of bed and started to make my bed, I would see these quotes and constantly repeat them to myself. Also putting little alerts in my phone that would practically go off all day long would send positive affirmations that would encourage me:

- You are unique.
- You are strong.
- You are beautifully made.
- Love yourself how you want someone to love you!

For a whole year, I repeated these four lines to myself. I learned that there is so much power and strength in the words that come out of your mouth. Not more than four months after starting this process, I found myself more confident in saying the quotes and believing what I was saying to be true. I also walked with my head held higher, and I had a boost of confidence in dealing with others. From doing this process, I built up the strength to do the unthinkable. I was ready to take on the challenge of focusing on myself and motherhood and becoming a better me, all before I entered into another relationship.

Some months later, while learning to navigate through motherhood, which seemed to consume all my time, I made time to date and spoil myself as well as understand some of the things that I liked and disliked. To be honest, this was a very interesting process because there were so many things that I liked that I didn't even know about. It was almost like I was discovering a new me! I didn't want to risk entering a relationship and possibly losing focus on the process I had already started. Not only that, but I believe that a relationship is a give-and-take thing.

I could no longer give what I was unable to give to myself (love, time, affection, happiness, etc.). I wanted to be sure to build and mold me the exact way I wanted, so when I was ready to enter into another relationship, regardless of how things went, nobody would be able to destroy what I had built in myself. I've learned quickly that what someone else builds up in you, invests in you, and so forth, they can also destroy in you. So if others put happiness in your heart or you didn't know love until they gave it to you, then when or if they leave that relationship, it's almost evident that they will take that love back so you will be left feeling incomplete without them.

The relationship I had with my daughter's father really broke me completely down. I had to reevaluate myself. I couldn't begin to figure out how to let him go. Most people would say, "To get over one fling, you should get under another fling." Now for me personally, I was pregnant, and I was not about to be sleeping around to heal an emotional feeling from one fling, only to open emotional baggage for another. There was the risk of putting my child in danger to only try to get a temporary fix.

Not only that, but how do you plan to release one thing for someone when you are filling yourself with countless other emotions? Understand that when sleeping with a man, he deposits a spirit, energy, and emotion inside of you. If you will be released, you have to be ready to release it all.

In August 2012, I knew I had changed for the better. I recognized it in myself. During this time, I knew who I was and what I stood for. I began to think about what brought me to this point, so I made an appointment with the same counselor. In the session, I told her, "Two years ago, you asked me who I was. I didn't know how to begin to answer that question, so I ran."

She responded, "But you're back. Do you know now who you are?"

In tears of joy, I was able to proudly answer her question. "Who am I? I am a strong, independent, vivacious, black Christian woman whose religious beliefs have broadened her expectation of what love is. I am a hardworking woman who strives to be a better child of God, mother, sister, daughter, friend, and, one day, wife. She has a smile that will lighten any tunnel and a personality that demands a level of respect with just her presence but still provides an essence of the sweetest and most unique aura. She possesses a great satisfaction in encountering other strong, successful women. I love who I was, what I am, and what I will become."

This is who I am, which took me over two years to be able to do some serious soul searching to realize some things about myself and the individuals I was allowing to consume my life. Take your time to learn you. Don't limit yourself to a time table or rush the process of trying to gain entry into a relationship. That will only lead you back to square one at some point. Do and complete this process now while you still have time, so when the right person for you comes along, you are not starting the relationship on a crutch of learning and building you.

Use the following questions to break down who you really are.

Questions

1. Who are you?

   _____

   _____

   _____

   _____

   _____

2. What are some things that you dislike about yourself?

   _____

_____

_____

_____

_____

3. Are you working to change those things you dislike?

_____

_____

_____

_____

_____

4. What are some things that you love about yourself?

_____

_____

_____

_____

_____

5. Do you make time for just you? If so, how?

_____

_____

_____

_____

_____

6. How do you know that you truly love yourself?

_____

_____

_____

_____

_____

⊰ **STEP 2** ⊱

CORE OF YOUR FOUNDATION

I don't think we typically think about the core or the base in which we build and stand on daily. I know that I never did. Once you become an adult and really begin to have a mind of your own and set short- and long-term goals for yourself, you really have to think about the foundation that are creating and laying for yourself. If you think of a house or a building that is being built, before you are able to lay the cement to be the foundation on which the house stands, you have to make sure the ground on which you are building is sturdy and leveled. If it's not level, the house will have no substance to stand firmly on.

That same concept applies to your life and your foundation (morals, standards, belief system, etc.). All these things work together to create the very essence of who you are. However, is the ground you are building your life on leveled? Is the foundation of your core existence lining up with who you claim to be? Regarding your morals, values, wants, and desires in life, are they formed, followed, and respected? They are what you set for yourself and actually live by.

So when someone comes into your life, it is almost natural that they will have respect for standards because what you are asking for is what you have already established for yourself. They are familiar to you, and you are not making them up as you go because you give it to yourself.

I mentioned in an earlier passage, "What you do to yourself, others will do to you as well."

Setting and living with morals, values, and so forth is not a bad thing. It's having an objective for your life. And if that is what you are living by and pouring into yourself, when someone else comes along and falls short of showing you that, you will begin to instantly distance yourself. That was my problem. I knew who I was and what I wanted, but I would compromise my morals and values to satisfy the needs of others or for what I thought I needed in my life. That is how I ended up entering a failed relationship and then a marriage that failed. You have to be consistent in learning, understanding, and forming yourself.

In the process before entering my marriage, there was a friendship as well as many years of dating. So I just knew that the way we were doing things was creating a firm foundation for our marriage to be built on. I learned one thing though. It doesn't matter how much work you do. If there is hurt or unhealed wombs that are not addressed, they will always leave bubbles in your cement as you lay the foundation.

I realize that was the importance of premarital counseling, to identify some things, work on a lot of things, and begin to build from everything. Sure enough, as we begin to build our marriage on this foundation, the marriages fail apart right before our eyes. Going through the process before we were actually married, I was so focused on me and making sure I was healed from any past hurt because the last thing I wanted was something in my past to affect my future. I didn't take the time to stop and make sure he was doing his necessary work and not just going through the process.

As women, it comes natural for us to want to do for others and be nurturing; however, at some point, you have to be selfish with your time and nurturing. Learn to nurture yourself, setting time aside and really engaging your feelings. We become accustomed to making sure that everyone around us is taken care of that we neglect ourselves. During the years I spent living in a different state, God isolated me from my family just enough for me to reevaluate myself, yet he provided me with some loving people so I didn't feel totally alone.

Some of our greatest life lessons are learned when we think we are at our lowest or when we have to endure pain. Crazy as it may sound, we tend not to learn unless our hearts are broken or on the verge of mental and physical destruction. You have to lose in order to gain and have to fall in order to grow. But it all things work together when becoming the person you are supposed to be. Notice, I never mentioned you have to compromise your standards or lower your values in order to be and get what you want in life.

While going through any situation, it will be unclear as to why you are going through it, but during this time, you are emotionally intact. Once your feelings are out of the way, you are able to see things a lot clearer. For example, if you sit back now and think about a previous relationship that you were in that ended, now that you're out of the relationship, you are able to point out all the red flags and the problems. But while in the relationship, you weren't able to because your emotions were involved.

Going through my marriage, I knew some things that were going on were wrong, but I didn't want to believe them or focus on them. So a lot was swept under the rug, I guarantee you. Those same things that were swept under the rug while we were dating are the same things that caused our failed marriage. If I would have held tight to the morals, values, and standards I set for myself, things would have been different. I probably would have never married this person, but I would have been able to identify things while they were happening versus looking back now and able to highlight them all.

I am a firm believer that everything happens for a reason; however, through everything, make sure that you learned something. An experience without a lesson learned is a waste of time.

Questions

1. What are some of your morals and standards?

   _____

   _____

   _____

_____

_____

2. What were the family relationship dynamics you experienced at home while growing up?

_____

_____

_____

_____

_____

3. What is one of your short-term goals?

_____

_____

_____

_____

_____

4. What is a long-term goal?

_____

_____

_____

_____

_____

5. What are you doing now that is working completely toward one of your goals?

_____

_____

_____

_____

_____

⊰ **STEP 3** ⊱

LEARNING TO LOVE ME!

During this process of learning to love myself, I found myself halfheartedly caring for others. I was giving a compliment but not really meaning it, or I was jealous of what someone else might have had that I didn't.

You must have time alone to learn to love yourself. Alone time is the only way you will learn how to do that. No one can demonstrate to you how to love you. You have to do it for yourself. People can only demonstrate how they love themselves, but until you learn to fully love you, you will always find flaws in someone else, which are really flaws within yourself. You'll never be able to give a sincere compliment or offer true happiness for someone else because of the imperfections within yourself.

We all have them. You may say, "I am too small or too big" or "I don't like my eyes, my nose, and so on." Even though we are quick to look at models on TV and say how perfect they are, there is still some type of imperfect qualities in them, whether they are noticeable to the world or just something from within. I would rather take my size, short hair, pretty smile, and strong personality over anyone whom I may feel looks better than I do. You really don't know what they suffer with personally that we may feel is so perfect.

You must also think about the imperfections seen, which are only magnified when you think someone else notices them or feels the same type of way about yourself. Most people are probably thinking something totally different, but because those are your insecurities, your mind takes you to those negative thoughts every single time.

We are so quick to put on makeup, extensions, and so on, only to cover up temporary or misperceived mishaps about ourselves. Don't get me wrong. Makeup, extensions, and all those things are perfectly fine, if you are sincere with who you are without all those things. I wear extensions simply because I don't feel like dealing with my hair or I want to wear a particular style I am not able to because of my natural hair length. However, I never use weaves as a permanent fixture. When I do wear one, I remove all of it when I come home.

Now on the flip side, I barely wear makeup or fake nails. I don't know how to wear it, and I don't like having all that stuff on my face, not to mention the time it takes every day to apply it. I rather not! I don't feel that I need that. I've been told many times that I have beautiful skin.

The point I am trying to make is that when you apply these things to yourself, understand why you are applying it. Women, I have heard so many men complain about meeting women. They can be one way, but it's like a whole different person behind closed doors. Who are you really fooling? Who doesn't want a man that accepts you as you are, with all of your marks, scars, and imperfections?

Every morning, I get up early and work out. It helps me start my day. There was a time when the thing I disliked about myself was that my knees bow inward. It's very obvious when I wear jeans. I prayed for confidence. I even toyed with the possibility of getting surgery on my knees. So one day while at the gym, I was undressing, about to get in the shower, and a young lady walked in. She was just smiling from ear to ear with a pleasant personality.

I then realized that her face was completely burnt, one eye was fake, and she was wearing a wig. We started having light conversation, and she shared that her children's father set her on fire because she was trying to leave him (which was an abusive relationship). Now let's start by saying that I thought stuff like this only happened in movies. She then shared that she was so happy because yesterday he was sentenced to life in prison without parole. She had been burnt so badly that when she cried, you could hear it in her voice, but the tears didn't flow down her face.

I instantly embraced her and heard the spirit of the Lord say, "Now what don't you don't about yourself?" I felt so silly. Here I was complaining about how my body was shaped, and this young lady was scarred for life. If she could smile and walk in confidence, why couldn't I? There was purpose behind me meeting this young lady.

So many times we complain about the small things instead of realizing there is a bigger picture such as life, health, and strength. We ended the conversation with her saying, "You are such a beautiful person with a memorable smile and huge heart. Never lose those."

I have met so many women who seem to fall short of actually loving themselves. You are beautifully and wonderfully made. Never let anyone disrespect or demean any of the characteristics of what makes you you. If you are in a relationship with someone who cheats on you and you continue to let it happen, there is not a problem with him. There is a problem with you.

As I mentioned before, I was a no go for any man cheating on me, no if, ands, or buts about it. It wasn't until I was in my marriage and I faced infidelity months after being married that I had to really understand what part caused so much hurt. Is it the actual cheating or continuous lies after you've been caught cheating red-handed? The denial of being caught and lying seems to hurt more than the actual cheating because he was making it appear like I fabricated the whole thing when I provided all the proof needing to show he was busted.

He was bothered that I went through his phone to find the information, in which I was totally wrong for invading his privacy, because my intuition was enough. The first few days it crushed me because I always assumed my marriage was better than that. After prayer and counseling, I decided to stay in the marriage, but I made it clear to him that I was hurt and he was not to do it again.

See, if you would have told me years ago that I would have been married and cheated on and then turn around and forgive my husband, I would have laughed in your face. My prayer was for God to soften my heart toward forgiveness and to help me to move past this.

Sure enough, God did that, and over time I wasn't as paranoid as I was in the beginning. So as you see, there was growth in me. I cherished my vow. That is why I put in the work. God helped me to realize that just because you are fighting for your marriage, it doesn't mean your values and morals are degraded. I believe that God was in the midst of my marriage; however, marriages require both individuals to pray, seek him, and do the work to keep it. In not doing all it takes, one can become deaf to God's voice and understanding, which can cause a marriage to spiral down to the point of no return.

To be honest with you, I would have to say the scariest part was witnessing my partner/teammate become so silent to who God is and getting in his presence at some point. Not even having the desire to pray or seek help is a terrible place to ever be in. We were both raised in the church and leaned on prayer as the main source to help different avenues of life challenges we may face. I began to see my marriage crumble right before my eyes. There was no respect and no sincere love. We were just going through the motions. There is a difference of doing for someone out of love and doing for someone out of requirement. It became so obvious that football was his love and I was a "chore" because he was my husband. We got through the infidelity, but then the disrespect, belittling, and emotional and the mental abuse started.

I remember crying out to God in pure shock like, "Okay, God, now I know that you are better than this with me being treated this way. What am I supposed to do? I have a little girl in the midst of this marriage."

It became my daily prayer that God would shield my daughter's heart, blind her eyes, and cover her ears to this type of behavior while I was seeking him for direction. Every day I woke and told her, "You are beautiful, you are loved, and you are someone special."

That is when I knew my transition had to begin. I was losing all respect for the man I married; his character was being demolished right before me. I asked

God to show me plain as day if I needed to leave this marriage, like I needed him to dummy it down for me so I had a clear understanding. Well, he did just that!

We had just came back from a family trip in Dallas with all my family, we went to the State Fair. While there my ex-husband would complain about making sure we were back in the hotel in time for him to watch the game. Things just seemed off the whole trip, but I did just that. Heading home from Dallas, he makes clear that he wants to watch the game that is coming on, so he is rushing home. As we arrive home, we enter the apartment to realize the electricity was off. I found that strange because I knew the bills were paid. He was so upset, so I begin calling and see what was going on and shortly after finding out there was an outage in the area. The company was not able to give me an estimated time frame as to when things would be back on, and just arriving home I wasn't sure how long they had been out. I stated to my ex-husband, we have a lot of meat in the freeze that I don't want to spoil, what if we take the food in the freezer to my parents, I'll cook you some food and you can watch the game there? He immediately stated no as he was changing his clothes. I reminded him that I don't want all this food to go bad, and I just had surgery on my wrist so couldn't carry more than ten pounds up and down the stairs. He made clear that he told me earlier that he wanted to go watch the game, and stated that he was going to the bar to watch the game. So sitting there with no electricity, I asked him so what do you want me to do with all the meat in the freezer? He responded with, "you figure it out, I told you I want to watch the game." As he prepared his bag, in the back room my daughter says, "Please don't leave." And moments later without hesitation he walks out the door.

My ex-husband left the house to go and watch the game at a bar. Upon returning home, I realized he didn't have on his wedding band.

I asked him, "Why aren't you wearing your ring?"

"I don't ever wear my ring!"

I chuckled. "Oh really? Since when?"

"I only wear my rings on special occasions."

"Oh, okay. What exactly are special occasions?"

"When I am with you or we are out as a family."

Laughing, "So then no one knows you are married, right?"

"I can get someone if I have a wedding ring not."

There you have it. I had my dummy-down moment because clearly this man thought I was the dumbest individual alive, to actually believe or think I would be okay with that. Not to mention we had the issue of him wearing his wedding ring the whole marriage, had counseling, multiple arguments, etc. He made clear after we were married that he doesn't like to wear jewelry, so that should excuse him from wearing his wedding ring.

He had disrespected our vows and me for the last time, saying things like, "I don't need you or this marriage," "If you're not happy, you can leave!" or, "your only good for sex and cooking my food!" or the best yet, "I can pull a woman whether I have on my wedding ring or not!" As if society hasn't already branded that sigma in a married women's mind, that there are thirty women on every corner willing and ready to break up a happy home, now I live with that reminder under my roof.

Now how would you know that unless you have tried pulling women with your ring on? I couldn't cry anymore. All I could do was laugh because this marriage had reached its all-time low. Not once did I have the desire to put him down as a man or his inability to lead this home, the marriage, and so on. God quieted my spirit so quickly (because we all know I was ready to go way left). I just said okay and finished cleaning the house. That night I began packing a bag for my daughter and me and headed over to my parents' house while I was figuring things out.

It wasn't just what he said. It shocked me more that he felt okay speaking to me like that and thinking I was going to be okay. That was the moment when I knew I had allowed my values and morals to be degraded for the pride and satisfaction of this individual.

My dad told me, "When a man shows you his true colors, believe it!"

I chose to choose myself over anymore hurt, disrespect, or emotional abuse. Nobody deserved to be treated this way, especially not me. A man should never have to tell you more than once that he doesn't want you. Learn to read between the lines or just listen and watch his actions. The way a man moves speaks louder than the words that come out of his mouth. A man who loves and values his women speaks volumes from his behavior, without him having to say anything.

See he felt that it was okay to speak to me like this, because this is how he spoke to all the women in his life if they disagreed with him at any point. I saw it, I disliked it, but I was certain he would never talk to me in that manner (crazy I know). So it's only natural for him to do what he has always been used to, and expect me to respond the way that he has been used to everyone else responding.

The point I am trying to make is that if you don't love and respect yourself, no one else ever will. You set the town as to how people will treat you, and what you will accept. People will treat you a certain way just because they know you will not do anything about it. Even the most perfect-looking person in the world will find something wrong with themselves. Embrace your flaws, we all have them. If you don't like it, then you change it, don't change for the betterment of someone else. I am here to tell you that you are beautiful the way you are, flaws and all. Nothing is more important than learning to love you the exact way you are. Those things that you dislike about yourself, someone else may love about you, embrace it. Stop making excuses for why you are the way you are and start working toward a better and new you.

Questions

1. Do you love who you are?

   _____

   _____

2. If you could change one thing about you, what would it be?

   _____

   _____

3. What is something you haven't accepted about yourself but you want someone else to accept about you?

4. What are some of your best qualities?

5. What makes you unique (different from the next person)?

❖ STEP 4 ❖

SINGLENESS

Before I dive into this chapter, let's come to a clear understanding about something. If you are not married, that means you are single. If you are dating someone, you are single. If you are engaged, you are single. If you are living together or in a common law marriage, you are single. So now that we have a clear understanding as to who needs to embrace singleness, let me begin.

The interesting part about this step is that no one ever really talks about living single or embracing their single life. You hear so much about dating, friends with benefits, engaged, or married. But how do you know how to do any of these things if you don't know how to live single? If you don't know how to embrace yourself, love on you, or be happy with you, one of the most important times of your life is when you are single because you are able to focus on yourself and fulfil your own purpose in life. When single, you don't have to think about taking care of or being a support system for someone else.

Often times people associate singleness with loneliness; however, those are two totally different things. How can you expect someone to enjoy your company or presence if you don't enjoy the company of your own? Or better yet, society has us thinking that you should be married with children by a certain age in order to have any purpose in life. Falling short of that means you are unhappy or, better yet, not enough. Let's take this time to really dive into what singleness consists of.

Being single can be a challenge when you are at a point in your life where you feel you are ready for a companion. You see I said, "When you feel." How do you know you are ready for a particular season in life when you haven't embraced every season you've encountered? Anytime you are faced with a season and you just bypass it, I assure you that seasons you bypass is what will defeat you at some point in the future. Every season of your life is important and provides valuable lessons for the upcoming season with the challenges you are about to endure, if you allow it to do such. Singleness is one of the most important times of your life; you must realize that when you are single, you are able to reach your fullest potential physically, mentally, and spiritually.

I will use myself as an example. After I found out that I was pregnant with my daughter, it took me three years to get over her father and work on me before I started dating again. That was a vital time for me because I was really doing the work to better myself, or so I thought. I would date. I was still dating on dating sites, entertaining the thought of a relationship. Even though I wasn't in an actual relationship, I put myself out there as if I were in pursuit of a relationship instead of embracing my singleness while working on me.

Now fast-forwarding my timeline, after filing for divorce, I was now sitting in the season of singleness once again, a season I didn't or couldn't embrace when I was in it the first time. You are not able to truly focus on your singleness if you are entertaining the possibility of a relationship. During your time of singleness, you have to minimize the time you give to dating, getting to know someone, and so on because you cannot truly get to know yourself if you are in pursuit of getting to know someone else.

When learning intricate parts of yourself, it is impossible for you to focus on you while entertaining the thought of knowing someone else. Embracing your singleness is learning all there is to know about yourself as well as learning to sit and love on the part of you long forgotten or placed aside. Learn what makes you happy, sad, or angry. Remember, the hobbies you love to do and what pushes you over the edge are a part of who you are. You can't ask someone else to accept something about you when you haven't accepted yourself.

A young lady who used to work for me asked how my first holiday was without my husband being there and how I managed. She was having a hard time with the holidays coming up and her boyfriend not being there.

I told her, "I am in a season of loving all over myself, every piece of me, making me happy. Unfortunately, with me doing that and being a single parent, I don't have time to sit and dwell on what was." I then asked her, "Do you believe in God and praying?"

She said, "Yes, and I did that."

I then inquired, "What do you like to do on your free time? What makes you smile?"

She stood there looking puzzled. So I told her, "Over this Christmas break, I want you to go out and have lunch or see a movie by yourself. Embrace and enjoy your own presence." I then told her that I wanted her to learn four things that she liked about herself or liked to do.

So when she returned to work after Christmas break, I asked how it went. "How was the lunch? What four things did you learn about yourself?"

She said, "I went to have lunch by myself, and I felt so weird. I just couldn't do it. I got up and left!"

I asked, "Why?"

"It didn't feel right. People were looking at me, and I just sat there and didn't know what to do."

The good thing is she was able to tell me two things that she learned she liked to do but couldn't think of anything else. In that moment, it dawned on me that this is the reality for a lot of people. So many of us have become accustomed to making sure that everyone else around us is happy and their needs are being met that we neglect our own. We don't feel complete unless we are surrounded by others to enjoy ourselves.

I can't begin to tell you how many women I know right now who are in a marriage only because they don't want to be alone or refuse to start all over. So they just deal with whatever. It really bothered me that this young lady felt so uncomfortable about having lunch by herself. Honestly, when I am by myself,

I have the most fun! I don't spend as much money, I can do what I want, and I don't have to consider what anyone else wants. Then I don't have to worry about entertaining anyone.

Let's be honest. This is all dating is, bringing entertainment to this outing for someone else. You plan a date that you think will satisfy them. While on the date, you are then constantly doing things and making sure they are enjoying themselves. Why not plan things for yourself? Why not entertain and enjoy yourself? There is way more satisfaction in self-awareness and self-gratification than anything else.

And so that is what I told her. "Until you are able to enjoy the presence of yourself, a man never truly will."

To me, that's the same thing as asking someone to do something you know you wouldn't do. If you wouldn't date yourself, why would you think someone else would? If you wouldn't take all measures possible to put a smile on your own face, why would you expect someone else to? Let's really consider what we are asking our companions to do for us. Not only that, but if you can't give yourself a 100 percent, how are you really able to give someone else the same?

That is why relationships end. It is difficult for a man to be with a woman who can only give him 50 percent or even 90 percent, especially when there is another woman around the corner who is dying to give him the full 100 percent. Ultimately you are cheating yourself because you have wasted time and energy in a relationship to end right back at square one, being alone and looking for love. Let's get it right now so in the next relationship entered, our morals and standards set for him will match those set for ourselves.

I've been asked so many times, "What am I looking for in a man?" Oftentimes I have answered it with a surface answer, someone who is tall, dark, and handsome. He has a job, is based in the Christian faith, and so on. I'd refuse to go too deep into my wants and desires in fear that man may not exist.

I would also make excuses of why that person may not meet my desires. I would say to myself, "No job? Well, he is looking. Not a Christian? Well, we can work on that!"

The list goes on, and that is too many excuses for what is ultimately unclear within you. I am sharing what I did because that is how crazy I was, trying too hard and finding love in all the wrong places. Because I didn't love myself, I was always going to be making excuses for the shortcomings of who I was with at that time. What you want is what you want, but you cannot ask for something that you are not yourself.

Think of it like this. If you were out and about and everyone had on their shirts in big and bold letters that stated what their flaws were, would you be more careful in which partner you chose? You have to remember in your choosing that what you get is based on the flaws listed on their shirts. Some might have a short list; other lists could be drastically longer.

Would you do the necessary work to make sure that the flaws on your shirt were short and few so passersby did not reject you? Be sure to be what you are asking someone else to be. I like to live by, "Treat me the same way you would want to be treated, not better, because then that would be unfair to you or asking you for too much." Nonetheless, if I respect you and treat you well, I should expect nothing short of that in return.

As I mentioned before, there are countless people I know to this day who are in a marriage or a relationship just to have someone they can call their own or dealing with craziness just so they don't have to start all over. One thing I've learned through experience is the more I put up with or accept, the more I am chipping away at my sanity and self-respect.

What will happen if the choice is made to remain in a relationship where you were cheated on, abused in some way, or simply just tolerated disrespect and so on? Once that relationship comes to an end (and it will eventually), you have to work twice as hard to rebuild and remold what you tolerated for so long. Before or while in a relationship, most people know if that relationship is for them, so why do we continue to waste valuable time? Your time, energy, and love are valuable. This should be how we view ourselves. I beg of you to value yourself in this manner, and once you do, you will meet someone who will understand and value you, your time, your presence, and your love just as much.

While on vacation, a friend called me just to have a vent session, sharing how she had gone through another failed relationship and was tired of men being such dogs. Then in the same conversation, she said how she was going on a dinner date with this dude that she just met one night at the club.

I stopped her as I asked her, "Do you think your relationship is really over? Are you going to allow time to get over one man before you jump into one with something else?"

She was silent for a minute. I could tell that her mind was pondering on something. All she could say was, "Nah, he is not a rebound."

Now you see I didn't say anything about him being a rebound. That is what she concluded, simply because that is a title that society has placed on someone who dates someone right after they have ended a relationship. You are never going to find the fulfillment you wanted from one person in the next person you get with. That will never happen. Bouncing from one relationship to the next, just so you don't have to deal with the scars of that previous relationship, it is a scary reality when you don't have to face the reality of being single, or, better yet, sit and deal with yourself. But what is even scarier is the baggage and weight you load yourself down with while trying to maintain and juggle all of this.

Having a failed relationship is a normal thing. What's not normal is taking the pain, hurt, or fear from one person and asking the next person to work through that. Would you want to enter a relationship and work through the hurt that they've encountered from the person before you?

True happiness is contagious; it's something that spreads like wildfire. Find and sit in your true happiness. I am a firm believer that you can show someone better than you can tell them. Why would you want to show someone how they should love you versus telling them? Why not become an example of what it should be?

Don't continue chasing after what it's not but appears to look like. At some point in time, you will have to face the relapse of multiple unfilled love quests that you have had to endure. I encourage you to deal with one at a time. Once you finish in a relationship, deal with that head-on and heal from that relationship before entering another.

Questions

1. What does singleness mean to you?

_____

_____

_____

_____

_____

_____

_____

_____

_____

_____

2. What are the morals and standards of yourself that you live by?

_____

_____

_____

_____

_____

_____

_____

_____

_____

_____

3. What are the morals and standards that you set to have in a companion?

_____

_____

_____

_____

_____

_____

_____

_____

_____

_____

4. What went wrong in your last relationship? Did you recognize and accept your faults?

_____

_____

_____

_____

_____

_____

_____

_____

_____

5. If you are in a relationship right now, are you happy with it? Are you just playing it safe in this relationship (scared to be alone/start all over, etc.)?

_____

_____

_____

_____

_____

_____

_____

_____

_____

_____

6. Get to know you.

_____

_____

_____

_____

_____

_____

_____

_____

_____

_____

    a. What do you like to do (hobbies)?

_____

_____

_____

_____

_____

_____

_____

_____

_____

_____

b. What makes you happy?

_____

_____

_____

_____

_____

_____

_____

_____

_____

_____

c. What makes you sad?

_____

_____

_____

_____

_____

_____

_____

_____

_____

_____

d. What is something new about yourself that you didn't know?

_____

_____

_____

_____

_____

_____

_____

_____

_____

_____

7. What does someone loving you consist of?

_____

_____

_____

_____

_____

_____

_____

_____

_____

_____

_____

❧ STEP 5 ❧

SLOW DOWN AND BE PATIENT

This step never really set well with me until I was single and able to sit back and observe how I was going through my life. I was so caught up in what television said. I began to think that the reality of a good life was seeing what others had and comparing it to what I was lacking. I wanted to speed up the journey I was on. Part of me wanted to have love, companionship, a best friend, and so on, and I wanted it right now. I also believe that me having a child so young caused me to want to rush the dynamics of what a family was, for not just my child, but also myself.

Personally, I made the mistake of looking for love in all the wrong places. I have really done some crazy things just to get a man's attention. However, when my daughter was born, I really took it hard on having a child out of wedlock and what that really meant. When I think about it all, I never imagined this for myself, my life, or my life's purpose.

Of course, instead of staying on the path God had for me, I took a detour that ended up in pregnancy and eventually with a little girl I would be raising on my own. I wanted so badly for my daughter's father to be there (as a family, not to co-parent). I wanted my child to experience a lifestyle like I had where both parents were happily in the home. Now in the process I wasn't thinking, *If I am married before even having sex and getting pregnant, then that lowers the chances of me winding up as a single mother.*

These were things that constantly played in my mind. I was wanting something. I was thirsty to chase after it. All the while, God was trying to get me to understand the purpose in what he is doing. Let me be clear. I am not saying that God's plan was for me to have a child in wedlock; however, it was necessary for me to have certain things happen in my life in order for me to become the individual I am today. Therefore, he knew I was to embark on this journey alone, only to be sure that I constantly leaned on him for guidance and understanding throughout this journey.

I think that every parent would like to give their child the best life possible and can only hope their child's life is never affected by selfish decisions we tend to make as adults, not thinking of how this one incident could possibly affect our future. I can say that I took the rough journey through life by simply not listening and not being patient. I knew as a young adult that one of my purposes in life is to be married and that my marriage would be a ministry to those who journey was similar to my own.

So since I knew that God has these specific plans for my life, I rushed the process and took matters into my own hands to ensure I got that life right now. I did not understand that I would only be getting a counterfeit of what he really has in store for me.

In the beginning, my marriage seemed like what I thought God wanted for my life. Of course, then choosing to marry what I thought was my forever husband (whom God designed for me), I wanted God to then put his blessings on what I accomplished. When things got really bad, I was looking for God to clean up the mess from what I brought together. If I were about to do a life-altering thing like marrying someone, I should have spent way more time in God's presence to get clarification, especially because I had a child.

Don't get me wrong. I prayed many times; however, I didn't stay in prayer long enough to hear back from God or get the okay. All stemmed from the ultimate lack of patience on my part. Sometimes I would ask God, "Why do you reveal so much to me if you know I lack the ability to be patient and live through your will for my life?"

This was the second time (the first time mentioned earlier) I heard God respond so quickly and so clearly. He asked, "Do you trust me? Do you trust what my Word says? Where is your faith?"

All three questions left me stumped because I trusted God but I wanted right-now results. I trusted his Word, but I didn't read it enough to apply it to my life or even my faith. I have a lot of faith, but it was just enough to get me where I needed for my life right now, not thinking about my future. To me, that's like taking a child to the candy store and telling them, "You can have two full bags of candy, but you can't have it right now. And I'm not going to tell you when you will get it. Just know you will get it." That child expects to have the faith and trust to believe that their parents will at some point very soon give them the candy they have shown them. Boy, that child would go crazy.

After I learned I made a decision based on that moment and not on my life as a whole, I realized God has a purpose behind everything he does. God was prioritizing things in my life for where I was going and not for where I was at that time. That is something we don't think about or realize when we make our own decisions.

As an individual, I wasn't ready for marriage or some of the requirements of marriage. I was yet to become leveled in my singleness in order to be able to be whole prior to entering into a marriage. As I look back, some of the disagreements and frustration all came from the inadequacy of my full potential. Constantly being paranoid about my daughter and how she was being treated was big for me. I wanted her stepfather to treat her as his own so she wouldn't feel a void.

I constantly watched my back, making sure I didn't set myself up, got hurt, or allowed myself to get played. Every time something with wrong, I couldn't say, "Well, God, you brought us to this. You will bring us through this."

But this wasn't God bringing us to. So I just had to pray and hope that God's mercy and grace would be with me through this time in my life. I later realized that what is for you will truly love and protect you. It will value you, your heart, and your fears as well as uphold your most sacred secrets, only to make sure they provide you with sufficient love that outweighs all of your past hurt.

Something else I learned quickly is when God puts his stamp on something, you don't have to worry about the mask that people have on around you, just to bless something they already knew shouldn't be. Individuals who pushed for our marriage, knowing it was not of God, surrounded me. I was hoping a miraculous act of God would shift things for it to be in his will, only because it was beneficial for that person that they wanted the best for. I was listening to man more than I was listening to God. Neither a man that is a servant of God nor his people will put their personal desires and preferences over the plan God has.

I can rejoice now because God knows me better than I know myself. As my Creator, he knows what my desires and wants are. I am a firm believer that if I am patient and live in God's will, I will get everything God has for me, which will end up being the desires of my heart.

Choosing to end my marriage was more exhausting mentally than anything else. I respected and cherished my vows, and in spite of what I did for personal fulfillment for that moment, I truly believe that God can turn any situation around. At first, that was my prayer request, that God would renew and remold both of us. However, it became very obvious that my child was suddenly a burden on the marriage, not wanting her around during times or always wanting to send her off. I was almost like this change came overnight.

After much prayer, counseling, and even more prayer by myself, I realized that my expectations were too high because I wanted God's ultimate miracle blessings on something I pulled together. I had to sit back and realize that is not how God works. I immediately went into asking for forgiveness and mercy over my life. I have heard many say, "God doesn't condone divorces!" I agree because it is in his Word; however, I had to realize quickly that God doesn't condone divorce of a union that he united. I kept seeing the end results of a marriage that I thought was God's doing. There were lies, deceit, and infidelity while we were dating, so why would I think all that would change once we got married?

Sure enough, months into our marriage, there were lies, deceit, and infidelity. My point is, pay attention to those red flags. Marriage is hard and takes work, but never to the point to where you are being belittled, mistreated, devalued, and so on. For me, that was the hard part because I found security and protection in him, only to see that I needed protection from him was a major slap in the face. It was necessary for me to get out of the marriage if I wanted to have an ounce of confidence, love, or value for myself. I began to feel myself being so unhappy and emotionally exhausted. This was an experience I wouldn't wish upon anyone.

I received forgiveness and peace over my situation to end my marriage fairly quickly and used much time to search myself and clarification from God on what I needed to move forward and heal myself.

Many people said, "You are handling this divorce so well" or "You are not sad!" That is because I have buried myself in God's presence and found healing. I didn't want this marriage to be something that hindered me mentally, emotionally, or spiritually. I knew I had done everything I could to fix it, and now my focus had to be put back on myself and remolding me. Also I found my closure in God, not man.

Oftentimes, we hold on for so long or fight even after walking away because we are looking for closure from this person. I knew that due to the type of person I was dealing with, I wouldn't get closure. My prayer was that God would provide me with a healed heart and answer any unanswered questions I had about my marriage.

Weeks later after choosing to leave my marriage, I realized I was asking for something that he wouldn't give to himself. With unconditional love, there is so much hurt and resentment there from past shortcomings. There's no way he loved himself and not work through that. I wanted him to love and be there for my child. He wasn't doing that for his own child, so why would he do it for a child that's not his? It's simple respect. Any person who cheats in a marriage lacks respect and value of themselves. At this point, I can't blame him for not fulfilling my request because I had unpredictable requests in this situation. I knew that going into the marriage and chose to ignore all of them.

Being patient, praying, and having quiet time will really help you navigate the direction your relationship is going in. Looking back over my previous relationship, I appreciate what God was providing me with. So many times, we say, "God, show me that this is not meant for me or that I am in the wrong relationship."

Then when your partner does something that shows us a red flag, we ignore as if it were just a one-time mistake. As a perfect example, I have heard so many times, "If you want to know how a man is going to treat you, watch how he treats his mama!"

Again, the infatuation of being in love blinded me. I wasn't paying attention to how disrespectful he was when he would talk to the women in his family over a disagreement or something or how he never recognized or embraced their feelings. So now here we are in a marriage, and he is talking to me and dismissing my feelings, the same way he did his mother. And I am sitting here confused as to why he would do this.

If a man cannot respect the woman who births him out her body, there is no way possible that will change for you. Any type of shortcomings arriving through childhood must be acknowledged, embraced, and concurred, or they will begin to be exposed in the relationship. This is just one example of many, but if I were patient and paid attention to the caution signs that God was giving me, I would have taken an easier detour through life that didn't have to result in a divorce.

Red flags are so important when dating and getting to know someone. I feel like many times God allows us to experience these red flags so you can see these caution signs bright and early. However, we tend to avoid them, thinking "I can change him," "It's not as bad as it seems, or even "He wouldn't do that to me!" That's one I used! Women should be treated just as such, like queens. At the same token, women, if we are requiring that we are treated like queens, that is how we need to conduct ourselves.

The only thing I could think about was what I was allowing to be exposed to my child. She was just a little girl. I beat myself up because this was what I thought I was so careful not to reveal her to. His family made sure to cater to the way he felt and avoid stepping on his toes in fear that he would isolate himself and not talk to them. When I began to see this spoiled behavior surface, I literally ignored it because I was not about to cater to his ego like his family did. I have never and never will belittle a man, but I also will not pump up your ego only to deflate me. Any man who would talk to a woman in that manner doesn't have respect for neither her nor himself. I encourage you to pay attention to the red flags as they happen. Trying to avoid them will only make it worse later.

Anything you have been through in life is never a mistake. It's a lesson. There are many things that college or books can teach you, but there is much more that experience can teach and show you. If you were/are in a situation where life is no longer what it was, take time to ask yourself some questions: What was my life like before? How did I get in that situation? What have I learned from it?

An experience without a lesson is time wasted. For many years, I felt that anytime something went wrong, it was God's way of punishing me for the choices I made outside of his will for my life. I used to really beat myself down because it was like, "What now? How are you going to get yourself out of this?"

After much time in prayer and seeking God for who he truly was, I realize the route my life had taken was necessary in order to frame me into what I am today. I had to take those wrong turns in order for God to produce the right turn. Now he can get the glory out of my life. He even broke it down for me a step further by showing me that if he gave me the perfect life, he would never get the glory out of it. He showed me that I had to go through something so he could bring me and show me who he was. He was revealing himself to me and showing he was greater than anyone or anything else in my life.

Questions

1. Why are you so impatient about being in a relationship/married?

    _____

    _____

    _____

    _____

    _____

_____

_____

_____

_____

_____

2. What was something you went through that you feel still clouds your
   judgment of life now? What did you learn from that experience?

_____

_____

_____

_____

_____

_____

_____

_____

_____

3. If you are currently in a relationship, what are some of the red flags that
   you have noticed?

_____

_____

_____

_____

_____

_____

_____

_____

4. What does love mean to you?

_____
_____
_____
_____
_____
_____
_____
_____
_____
_____

    a. What is the difference between love and lust? (Oftentimes we don't understand the difference until we have written both down and compared them to our current situation.)

_____
_____
_____
_____
_____
_____
_____
_____
_____
_____
_____

✧ STEP 6 ✧

PARENTING OVER EVERYTHING

I want to begin this chapter with applauding any and every parent who takes the necessary time to make sure that your child is taken care of mentally, physically, financially, and emotionally. So let's being by clearing some things up, women. You are not a baby mama! You are a mother who has chosen a journey without the child's father. Men, you are not a baby daddy. You are a father who has made the conscious decision to raise this child outside of a relationship with the mother. Many of us put ourselves in a category of baby mama, which comes with the connotation of "She must be crazy!"

No one goes into a situation with a plan of only being a baby mama or a single father. It's just an unfortunate situation that turns out as such. It takes a strong woman/man to actually raise their children alone (whether the other parent is in their lives or not) and make necessary moves to make sure that your child is taken care of. However, I think there is a misunderstanding of the actual role that parenthood entails because we have altered what's needed with personal desires. In my opinion, this causes all single parents to look a certain kind of way, mostly negative.

Some of us may receive child support, and most fathers tend to think that money is enough support. However, no one thinks about the sleepless nights, sick days home from school, game days, or midnight nightmares. All of these require being there but have no bearing when it comes to financial support. Having a child is a lifestyle change, not just the financial responsibility. Raising a children can be mentally and physically exhausting if necessary measures on both parents' parts are not taken. I have encountered some men who feel that paying child support is enough or will keep the baby mama happy and quiet, not focusing on what all a child will need in their lifetime. I have also come to realize that the source of a lot of men not being in their child's life is due to behavior and stresses that come from the mother.

Please understand me clearly. In my mind, there is nothing anyone can do that would affect me from being in my child's life, and I am not saying that this is the only reason. However, most mothers tend to hold all the cards when it comes to the child, and we tend to make things hard and impossible for men because of personal resentment, anger, or even jealousy. As grown women, we have to handle the two issues separately.

That was the hardest thing for me to do because I wanted to hurt him just like he hurt me; however, the only person who was truly getting hurt was my daughter. As mothers, we have to do things that are in the best interest of our children because what will begin to happen is our child will start acting out or begin to be resentful of the relationship you have. I truly believe that more men would be in their children's lives if women didn't make it so hard for them. Or better yet, if both parties would equally do their part, the system would be the determining factor in so many lives.

Society has changed the order of how things used to be, which was marriage first and then children. If you are one who has children prior to entering a relationship, your children come first. If you are in a relationship with a man who is not your husband and you already have children, your children always come first. Truthfully, any man of integrity would respect that and want you to put your kids before him until he is man enough to marry you. Then once marriage comes into play, the love, respect, and passion is there for you and your children and naturally has no problem putting your new husband before your children. What happens then is you and your children will become his first priority.

I have seen many times where I have observed relationships when the woman has been so caught up in this relationship that she fell off being a mother. Her main priority became the man, and her total focus was on the relationship. In making those types of adjustments in your life, the children tend to suffer from the constant transitions when a new man or woman comes around. The way you are with your children while you are single should be the same way you are when you are in a relationship. That is why when you are a parent, you should not be bouncing from relationship to relationship. Each relationship you get in you is giving a piece of yourself to that person. (I am referring to mentally, emotionally, physically, and, let's not forget, sexually.)

So each piece of your time or love that you give to a relationship is time and love taken away from your children. Of course we all think we have enough love to go around for everyone, but at some point in your life, you have to be a little selfish and cautious as to who gets to experience your love. Not everyone is deserving of that. Any person who wants you to put them before your child is not the individual for you. Learn how to transition through life with the lifestyle you have created for yourself. Learn to be happy and complete with just you and your kids, so that when you do add someone into your life, it's just added love instead of added heartache or problems.

I have seen so many situations where women are so caught up in the men in their lives that their children begin to come second or even third priority. To take it a step further, once I got a glimpse of parenting, my whole world seemed to transition, focusing on my mental state to be sure I was able to provide for my child as needed. What I am saying is my first priority instantly became my daughter. My daughter never met anyone I was dating until I was for certain the relationship was going toward marriage. I am referring to time spent to know and learn this individual, coming to terms on the direction this relationship was going, and actually going that route. Not just thinking I was in love, but actually months and years of consistency from this man.

Most people would say, "The dude I am with needs to meet my children so I know if he really likes kids or if my kids like him."

Here is the thing. I don't care what a man tells you. Everything that comes out of his mouth in the first six months could be a straight lie. So if he tells you he likes kids and then behaves a different way, what good does that do? The instinct of any parent, especially a mother, is being able to identify a person's sincerity when it comes to kids, that is, if love has not already blinded you being able to see things clearly.

When a person really has a passion for children, that side of them will show whether they meet your children or not, from their patience to respect for your time and mindfulness of you having children. For me, it was important for me not to have that introduction while dating because what my child thinks and feels is ultimately the most important thing to me.

Having a little girl who is so sensitive to the possibility of receiving love she desires from her father daily, I had to guard her diligently to make sure she wasn't affected behind my actions. The men she is raised around determines how she views men. For her, that was my father and her uncles, who have all demonstrated the qualities of a great fatherly role model in her mind. I would never want to tarnish that thought for her with a "possibility" that I feel may be a permanent decision. I never wanted my child to see multiple men in and out of our lives. To me, no one had any significance in her life unless it was someone who would be there permanently.

My ex-husband and I built a friendship for years. He was aware I had a child but never met her. Even after we started dating and became intimate, still he never met her. I made sure to do whatever was necessary to separate my wants at the time with the priority of protecting my child from the "what ifs." It wasn't until about two years later that I made arrangements for the meeting between them to take place. When I introduced them, I was able to be honest with my child and tell her this was someone whom Mommy really cared about, not her uncle, not my friend, and so on.

I've created a relationship with my child where we are able to be open and honest with each other about everything. To be honest, that was the best thing I could have ever did because after having him as a father figure in her life for almost three years, I was able to be honest with her when choosing to end my marriage by letting her know that things would be changing.

I agree with the point that children shouldn't know all of grown folks' business, but I think it is important that we are honest with ourselves first and then with our children so they understand the reasoning behind the things we do. What you don't make clear to a child will only be filled with justifications they make up for themselves. I value myself too much to have men coming in and out of my home. Not only that, but that is not the type of young lady I am trying to raise my daughter to be.

As women, we choose whom we want to be in a relationship with, whether it was a good decision or not. The children we raise don't have the option of choosing who their parents will be, so that is why they should be held in the highest priority after being brought into this world. There are many men out there who will raise another man's child just like they are their own. That alone is very commendable; however, some men will pretend to like your child just to get in good graces with you.

Your children should not become the responsibilities of another man (who is not their father) until he has (man up enough) put a ring on your finger. Leaving your child in the presence of a man who is not her father should not be an option until you have taken all necessary measures to ensure your child is okay with this person alone. Boyfriends are not babysitters. Even if they offer, of course it's easier and probably even cheaper; however, the safety and well-being of your child is far more important. I was molested as a child, so I made sure that I didn't even allow the opportunity of something like that happening to my daughter.

One of the jobs as a mother is to ensure the physical, mental, and emotional safety of your child. Thinking that you know someone because you have been with them for months is not enough to ensure your child's safety. It breaks my heart seeing on the news or hearing stories where mothers have left their child with the boyfriend and the boyfriend then beat, killed, or molested that child. And a lot of times these things happen to the child because of the frustration the boyfriend has toward the mother. The wants or temporary desires for you or a man should never take precedence over your child. To be honest, any man who asks you to put him before your children is not a man. A true man understands your obligations to your children are first because the children were there first. He can get on board to help or step aside. But until he has positioned himself as a man of purpose and put a ring on your finger, he has no say whatsoever.

This leads me into my next thought. What time frame do you think is good enough for your child to meet someone you are dating? Allow that question to soak in for a minute. I heard people say that they need to meet them immediately to see if they even like the children or how your children feel about him. I have also seen relationships where the children were introduced a month into the courtship. This seems to be rushing the process as they are placing the children in a position to risk their hearts, having family outings and everything.

Here is the thing. You will learn a lot about a person by just sitting back and quietly observing them. As adults, we are expected to have more experience and the ability to identify the qualities and flaws of an individual. We should have more insight than our children do. Therefore, your children shouldn't be meeting every person who is in the dating category. You are dating because this is someone whom you are learning and figuring out for yourself. So why put your child in the mix of that until you know this is something more than someone you just hang out with?

Dating is just that, collecting data and doing the work before investing your children's hearts. They are affected when changes are made too quickly. You may not see it now, but it will come out as they grow and mature. Your home is your safe place, and it should definitely be your child's safe zone. Your home should not be where random traffic should be open to.

I will use myself as an example. Before I got married, I never brought anyone into my home where my child lives. After my marriage was over and I started dating again, I still would not bring men to my house. That is where my daughter feels the safest, and I would never want to hinder her ability of feeling that way. Don't get me wrong. Some men can have the best intentions for you, your child, and your home, but why not allow time to make certain?

For me, it's not even about making sure not to bring the opposite sex in my home. I don't have a lot of traffic in my home, period. When you have too many people in your home, they might have different spirits and possible demons attached to them that could possibly be left lingering in your house. A lot of my associates or friends don't come to my house. We go and hang out, or I will go over to their place. My home is an area of love, peace, and security, something I want it to always remain. I care about how my daughter views me, and I never want her to think that it's okay to have multiple men coming in and out of our house. To this day, she will tell you, "My mom doesn't like too many people over at our house!"

Child support is financial assistance from one parent to the child and for the child and their custodial parent to help on a consistent base. Many men don't like the idea of giving money to the mother (who tends to be the primary parent) because they feel those funds are not being used properly. This is really an ongoing situation. I heard this debate from both sides. The individual paying the child support felt the money was being used on the upkeep of the custodial parent's physical appearance. Yet the custodial parent felt that money could be used for what they want to use it on.

Unfortunately no law tracks and monitors the way each dollar is spent from child support. But I understand both sides of the situation. The noncustodial who is paying child support has a right to question what money is being spent on if they see a problem. Women, I don't understand for the life of me how you are getting child support. Your children look halfway decent, and you receive countless government services. There's no college fund for the children, and they are constantly in the streets.

Something needs to be reevaluated about your life. Government assistance are for those individuals who really need assistance for that time being, not people who want extra help so they don't have to use their own funds or child support money on rent, groceries, electricity, and so on. We have to start taking accountability for our own actions. When having these children, be ready to do what's necessary to take care of these children we so freely have.

Now on the flip side, I don't see anything wrong with a custodial parent taking $40 out of her child support money to get her nails done or whatever. If all the bills have already been paid from her income, groceries are in the house, and your child is set, then why can't they? All of these things come with a balance and understanding what the main focus is, the child's needs.

As mothers, if we change the way we do things, then these fathers will begin to feel differently when it comes to financially taking care of their children or even being in their lives. I am not saying that is the reason most fathers don't take care of their children. I am merely stating we could do better as well. I am not a man, so that is why I want to focus on us as women.

With the kind of society we live in now, we have to start taking accountability for our actions. We must start openly communicating with our children, and most importantly we have to remain the parent and allow them to remain children, not our friends or fill-in companions. Children are children for a reason. Their minds are only able to tolerate and comprehend so much. We have to remember that when putting too many expectations on them or treating them like they are adults. Let's fully understand what a mother (parent) is and what our primary goals are.

Questions

1. What is something that you love about being a parent?

_____

_____

_____

_____

_____

_____

_____

_____

_____

2. What does being a parent mean to you?

_____

_____
_____
_____
_____
_____
_____
_____
_____
_____

3. As being a parent, does your child's needs/desires take precedence over your needs/desires in life? To what extent?

_____
_____
_____
_____
_____
_____
_____
_____
_____
_____
_____

4. What is the time frame in which you think it is okay to introduce your children to the person you are dating? Why do you feel your child should meet every person you date?

_____
_____
_____
_____

_____

_____

_____

_____

_____

5. If you went back and evaluated all of your relationships (when your child was involved), what do you think your child learned, gained, or remembered from that relationship?

_____

_____

_____

_____

_____

_____

_____

_____

_____

_____

   a. What would you have done differently?

_____

_____

_____

_____

_____

_____

_____

_____

_____

_____

❧ STEP 7 ❧

FULFILLING YOUR PURPOSE

In this chapter, I had to remain in prayer for a while because this is a little close to home and was a touchy subject. The importance of your purpose and the plan that God has for your life, I don't take that lightly at all. So I wanted God to direct me step by step in this area, so I made sure what I was saying was lining up with his will.

Each one of us was born with a purpose. So here we have it. You have built a solid foundation within yourself as to who you are and what you stand for; therefore, when standing for your purpose, you have the ability to stand in confidence and not easily be distracted by others.

The importance of you fulfilling your purpose is critical for someone else. God allows things in our lives to happen, not just for you or to make you stronger, but so this will help someone else. Your purpose works the same way, filling it to benefit others, not just yourself.

So think of it like this. Someone is sitting there (possibly losing their mind) waiting for you to fulfill your purpose and provide them with something no one else but you can give them. We think it's not that big of a deal. Someone else can help them. But God has this set up like a spider web. You are connected to someone and don't even know it until you have fulfilled your purpose. Take your time and look at the diagram below.

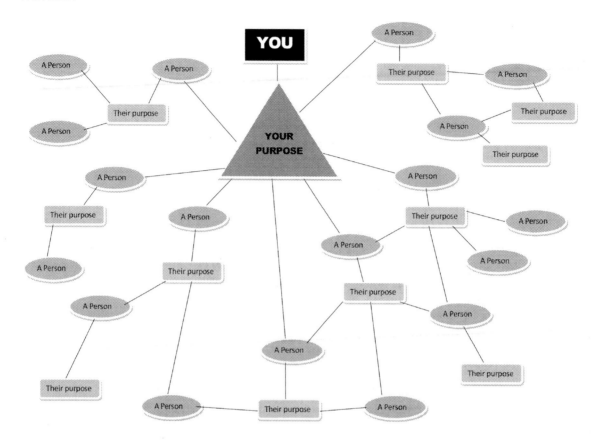

When looking at the diagram and seeing where you are positioned, there are individuals who are attached to you through your purpose. Then there are other people who are attached to their purpose. It is an ongoing thing. Everyone has a purpose that others are waiting for to be fulfilled. Just think about how many people could possibly be connected to your purpose and waiting for it.

You don't know how many people are connected to your purpose or how many you are affecting if you don't fulfill your purpose. Or they are struggling through life, and your purpose brings them a sense of peace and understanding. It wasn't until God showed me this example of a diagram that I began to diligently seek him for my purpose because I wanted others to get their full potential out of life. I refused to allow it. To me, that was a blockage for them because I didn't do my part. Not only that, but God is going to hold you and me accountable for every person who was attached to our purpose, which never fully manifested.

You are able to fulfill your purpose while being single. Many people think you must have a spouse in order to understand or walk into your purpose. Not true! This is why singleness is one of the most important seasons of your life. It allows God to get your full attention and potential without any distractions. You don't have to worry about being a wife, husband, mother, father, and so on, and you are able to put all your attention into fulfilling your purpose. Marriage is not a journey that should be taken to fulfill or justify our lives.

If it were God's plan for you to only obtain your purpose once you are married, then a lot of people would have never moved in their purpose due to marrying someone that God never intended for them. You must be complete before you enter a marriage. Your level of singleness will show and affect your married life if not embraced and sought out fully.

So many people are married (and have been a long time), and they are having marital problems and just can't seem to get it right. That is a singleness problem, not a married issue. Don't misunderstand me. There can be a purpose attached to your marriage because marriage is ministry. However, each person has their own individual purpose in life. I have learned through experience that if you are a damaged person (in any way), you will begin to make excuses for not reaching your purpose. Not seeking God for understanding, purpose, and so on or not having the desire to pursue your purpose is just another excuse after excuse. Your purpose cannot fully flourish until you have been healed from being damaged.

I have a clear understanding as to what my purpose is, and this self-help book is part of me completing my purpose. It took me a while to accept the purpose God had on my life because I felt like people would prejudge me or feel like I didn't know what I was talking about due to my age. However, there have been many times when someone I know has reached out to me about personal problems they were going through and wanting to vent, trying to understand certain things. And God just had me silent and showing me, "See, this one could have used your book. There's another who would benefit from your book!"

Then I had to realize. What if the healing I once needed in my life was attached to providing a sequence of purpose in someone else's existence? Would I still drag my feet on fulfilling my purpose?

Questions

1. Have you diligently sought after God regarding your purpose?

_____

_____

_____

_____

_____

_____

_____

_____

_____

_____

2. What is your purpose?

_____

_____

_____

_____

_____

_____

_____

_____

_____

_____

3. What past/present damage is affecting you from fulfilling your purpose?

_____

_____

_____

_____

_____

_____

_____

_____

_____

_____

4. If you are fully aware of what your purpose is, what are you doing right now to fulfill your purpose?

_____

_____

_____

_____

_____

_____

_____

_____

_____

_____

5. Have you embraced your purpose, or are you leery and uncertain about it?

_____

_____

_____

_____

_____

_____

_____

_____

_____

_____

6. Who are you surrounding yourself to that is causing you to silence your purpose?

_____

_____

_____

_____

_____

_____

_____

_____

_____

_____

Something to Think About

There are many married people who choose to remain in their marriage because it has turned into a business relationship. There isn't an ounce of love there, but they feel it's better to stay married than to go through the trouble and embarrassment of a divorce. If children are involved in the marriage, the focus is so much on the children that they become a distraction to the real problems or issues within the marriage.

Something to keep in mind is, once the children leave the nest, those same problems will begin to manifest all over again, and the couple are back at odds. A lot of problems that will surface in a marriage are not really marriage issues. They are problems within your singleness. If you did not embrace and live out your season of singleness, I guarantee you that it will surface in your marriage. I am saying this from experience.

There are things I needed from my ex-husband that he could never give to me because I never gave those things to myself. Two individuals must understand and live in full completion of their singleness in order to have a productive marriage. Everyone is so excited to get married; however, no one realizes that marriage will expose the hidden, incomplete areas of each of your lives prior to them becoming one.

If you are a broken individual who will be exposed once you get married, it's necessary to heal your brokenness while still single because two people coming together who are both broken only create a foundation of unsteadiness to build on. Trying to heal brokenness in a marriage (even if only one person is broken) creates distractions in the marriage. It takes time from the possible growth of the marriage to focus on making sure you're healed.

Other than God, there is no one or no one thing that someone can do that can heal and restore your brokenness. So many times we feel that if we are in a relationship, we will use it as a distraction and not deal with what the real needs and issues are. So we push them aside and never deal with them. In the beginning, things may be great, but at some point, the broken parts of you, the things you have covered up, will begin to show, and you will have to reveal it.

I think of it just as makeup. We wear makeup to cover up some things, whether they are scars, acne, and so on, or to give ourselves a fresh look. When in a relationship with someone, there will be a point in time when that person will see you without all that makeup on, and they will see what you really look like. At some point, you are going to get tired of having hid who you are in order to maintain a successful relationship.

Imagine the level of happiness, peace, and love you would be able to live if both you and your spouse are whole. If you are married, you can still find healing for yourself. It's a little more difficult because it's not just you. It's very possible for healing to be done.

All Men Are Dogs

I knew this title would catch your attention! It's an interesting topic! So true, huh? I am glad that someone is in agreement with me. Is that what you are thinking right now. I hate to be the bearer of bad news, but women are dogs too, and no, not all men are dogs.

When you think of a dog that is stranded and sniffing around for food, if someone offers food to that dog, what will happen? The dog will slowly approach that person and then begin eating the food. Not only that, but the dog then begins to linger around because he could obtain some of what he needs from that person (food).

So if the men are the dogs, what does that make you? The individual providing food for that dog! Why are you feeding lost and strained dogs? If all men are dogs, why are you entertaining them? Here's the thing. I don't think that all men are dogs. I may think that men have doggish tendencies, but I also think that you may be picking men who are dogs. If that is what you keep choosing, of course it will seem like all men are dogs!

I used to feel all men were sneaky, stinky dogs. I went through life thinking that all men were the same way, simply because that was all I had experienced. It wasn't until I ended things with my daughter's father that I realized something in me was attracting these kinds of men. These men were not so much dogs, but they were doing what came natural to them, to sniff until they found what they wanted, me or the female standing next to me. I had morals and standards, but I was always willing to bend them in order to find happiness. It was not until after I spoke with some of my guy friends and heard what they were going through with their girlfriends that I realized that both and women could be so called "dogs." That's generally a name associated with men in order to justify them treating us so badly.

Your outlook on others will never change until your outlook on you has changed. Typically we are able to identify certain characteristics or flaws in others because we are afraid to identify within ourselves. We have all done some things to people we care about that that we are not too proud of. If you don't like the things or people you are attracting, you need to look in the mirror before doing anything else. Even if you leave that person, you will still attract the same qualities in the next, and you will still feel the same way you do after a while.

If you want something different for yourself, then you will need to do something different. I urge you to stop and fix it before you cause yourself anymore heartache.

STEP 8

TRUE FORGIVENESS

I have heard many people say, "Forgiveness is for you, not the other person." That statement is true, but I like to take the process a step further. How do you expect to receive what you are afraid to go for? One of the main reasons I put together this self-help book is because this was the process I completed myself once I decided to end my marriage. Any relationship that you end there tends to be some kind of resentment, bitterness, or hurt from that person. These issues can later cause you to search for and pick out those same distasteful qualities in the next relationship.

Whether you are the one ending a dating relationship or marriage (legal or common law), it is not healthy for women to leave one relationship to only enter another one. There are necessary things that you were to learn in that relationship, and if you don't take the time after ending that relationship to go back, acknowledge, review, and rebuild, you will carry that same baggage from one relationship into another.

As women, it is important that you focus on and nurture your feelings, emotions, and heart more than anyone else's. Doing so will allow you to rebuild once someone has broken it. Will the process be easy? No. However, it will be easier than waiting for someone new to put together what someone else has broken. I have met many women who really didn't know themselves until they entered into a relationship, and then it was like this man taught them how to smile and what they liked. They taught them to be happy, love, live, and so on.

When you give somebody that much control over your life, it will only allow them to have that same power once they decide to break your heart.

I have been in relationships where I was looking for love from a man because I lacked love in other areas of my life. He had to do many things in order for me to be happy, and if he didn't do it, I was miserable. I needed these individuals to make me happy so I could function on a daily basis. The process of ending the relationship and having to move on was always hard for me. I allowed him to build me up to only knock me down. If he didn't build me back up into who I felt I could not be, that was when I realized I didn't have the ability to do that myself.

My eyes were not fully open until I decided to end the relationship with my child's father and focus on myself. My daughter's father was the first man I ever truly loved. He had my heart wrapped up in his hand. However, there was still something missing in the relationship, but I couldn't seem to figure out what it was. However, I knew I wanted to raise my daughter with the right mind-set, as well as be the best example of how a woman should love herself.

There was a lot of hurt after I made the decision to end our relationship because I didn't like some of the changes he was going through in his own life. I did not like that his future child and I were not being included in his life. I didn't want to go into parenting having to juggle a new relationship; therefore I told myself that I would take time to learn about my new role as a mother and myself. I knew that when it was time, real love would come.

It took years for me to open up about the way I felt about my daughter's father. He was stationed in another state, so I didn't have to deal with seeing him and reliving those feelings on a daily basis. Not only that, but because I chose not to be in a relationship with him, he also chose to act as if I didn't exist, not realizing that he would be hurting his child as well. Because I didn't work through those feelings, I began to resent him for not being in our lives. My hate for him only worsened.

In the midst of me disliking him, I didn't say anything about him to my daughter or around her. I made sure that whatever she felt about him came from her own experiences from him. I remember telling him over the phone, "If you and your child don't end up having a relationship, it will be because you didn't want it."

It literally took me five years to learn to accept him for how he was and forgive him for all the hurt in the past. It took a lot of praying, opening my heart up, and revisiting those feelings. Because I realized that even though I didn't have anything to do with him for those years, any relationship I would have gone into, I would have had resentment toward any man because of what my daughter's father did. That is why I am a firm believer of the saying, "Forgiveness is not for the other person. It is for you." Unforgiveness is extra luggage used to weigh you down, which leaves you holding the grudge.

I forgave him for the hurt, and I took on the role of mommy and daddy. My prayer was that God would build him up to become a better parent and to open my heart for when the day came when he would want to be back in his daughter's life. I knew that it would come. I just didn't know when. Sure enough, seven years later, he began calling, visiting, and being active in her life.

In all of that time, I never defamed who he was as my daughter's father. She was right there, ready to accept him with open arms. The hurt he did to me had nothing to do with her, so why cause friction in their relationship because I was bitter? When he decided to come back, I didn't bombard him with third-degree questions as to where he had been. All I knew was that he was there now, and I wanted to give my daughter the opportunity to experience and embrace her father's love whether it would only be for a day or the rest of her life. I made sure to applaud him any and every time that he came around, as well as letting him know that I would do anything I needed to help create and build their relationship between father and daughter.

A lot of times, as women, we want the men to relive the past to get a glimpse of what we went through, but the truth of the matter is that they never will. Women were made the way they were for a reason. We are able to carry a human life inside of us for months. Just like there are things we can do, there are also things that men can do things that we cannot. There are things we can do and were made to handle specifically for the purpose of being nurturing.

I take pride in knowing that my household cannot be run properly without me in it. Yes, a father can take care of the child if you have to go to work or take some time out to be with friends, but can most men do what women do as single mothers on a daily basis?

Learning to forgive allowed me to be a better person, mother, and friend to what is going to be. Holding on to grudges for all those years only held me back and made me resent certain things about men altogether. Nevertheless, I am able to see my daughter's father through a new light. We have both grown up and become a little wiser as adults and parents, and both of us have the same end result of doing what was best for our child.

Learning to forgive him helped me to learn not to harp on things and to move more freely in releasing unnecessary baggage. Forgiveness is a beautiful thing when done correctly and effectively. Life is so much better and happier when you are not weighed down with hate and anger for someone who probably doesn't even matter anymore. The true test of forgiveness comes in two different ways:

1. When you are able to pray for that person and be sincere in your prayer. Excluding you and truly going to God in prayer for that person, it's an exhilarating experience when you have so much peace in your life and you know that God is going to bless you. You know you are free when you can intercede for someone who has caused brokenness and unhappiness in your life. The reward to all of this is knowing that you have also been able to deal with your own brokenness from the past.
   - I have always prayed for my marriage, and then when it ended even through the hurt and misunderstanding, I still prayed for my ex. During the marriage it was prayer of fixing the situation, giving me patience, giving me understanding, opening his mind and hurt, etc. During the separation it was prayer for guidance for both of us, healing for both of us and for him from pass hurt that took precedence in our marriage. Then prayer for closed for both of us, and that wherever our futures lead us individually, that this

marriage would have been a lesson and not heartache, and provide growth and knowledge to every future situation.

2. When you are able to see that person and talk to him from a loving and sweet place. Whether it's having a full conversation or just being cordial, you are functioning in love. For me, I had to really think about how I was going to be able to function in love with someone I was upset with. I also had to think about the love and forgiveness that God gives us. Countless times I have hurt him or betrayed him, and each time he forgave me with open arms and still showers me with unconditional love. As children of God, we have to learn to function in that same love. Once I chose to really end my marriage, I immediately went into prayer for my husband. Not that I wanted him to get it right for the marriage, but I wanted him to get it right for himself, his life, and his future. This was someone I truly cared about and didn't want him to suffer unnecessarily. One of the scariest things in life is a believer (someone who knows God) deliberately running from God. They no longer fear who God is or what they do to God's people. They do not care about who is hurt, who knows, or who tries to help. Isolation will only prolong the time in which you are completely healed. Again, being able to transition in life, face different obstacles, and still have the ability to pray and love people will really elevate your level of understanding and ability to trust God in everything.

-   I have seen my ex-husband since the divorce while he was working. To be honest, I felt nothing, I was glad to see that he appeared to be doing well, but I continued with what I was doing. I've even shared with him times before during the separation that I truly want nothing but pure happiness for him, and that wasn't something I could give to him, and I except that.

It is fine to reminisce, but if you reminiscing causes you to relive, redo, or reinact, you don't need to reminisce. You can forgive and not forget, you can wish happiness for someone and not want to rekindle what was. There are things that God wants to do for you and through you; however, holding on to past hurt, resentment, and anger will only cause a delay in your life's journey. So many times we venture off the path God wants us on. If we had remained on our journey and stayed within his plan, we would have some of those things by now. Because we want things faster than we should, God has to make sure we are ready mentally and spiritually before he releases certain things in our lives.

Questions

1. How has not forgiving someone affected your life/emotions?

_____

_____

_____

_____

_____

_____

_____

_____

_____

2. Who do you need to forgive? And why?

_____

_____

_____

_____

_____

_____

_____

_____

_____

3. Why is it hard for you to forgive this person?

_____

_____

_____

_____

_____

_____

_____

_____

_____

_____

4. If this person apologized to you, would you be able to forgive them? Why or why not?

_____

_____

_____

_____

_____

_____

_____

_____

_____

_____

Sometimes as women, we just want the other person to realize that the things done and said, the wrongs, simply hurt us. We feel that this would bring us closure. Whether you get an apology from that person or not, you have to let go of the hold it has on you. So for that sake of helping you through this, this allows me to be that individual for you. What is it that you need to say to me to release you from the bondage they have over your life? Forgive them.

"I, [their name], want to apologize for any and all the hurt I caused toward you. I apologize for not realizing sooner that I hurt you and acknowledging your feelings. Lastly, I apologize for my selfish ways and not correcting the hurt I caused. Please forgive me!"

Whether you get an actual apology from this person or use what I have said to begin your healing process, move beyond this for yourself.

HAPPINESS AFTER DIVORCE

Anyone who has experienced a divorce of any sort has gone through a great deal of mental and emotional exhaustion. Therefore, it is very important that you focus on you when coming out of a marriage before you ever start thinking about dating again. No one deserves to be a rebound or have to deal with the hurt and brokenness from another person.

For me, once I decided to leave my ex-husband, I knew the marriage was over because I had spent much time in prayer and trying to make it work. Once I officially moved out, I immediately began working on me. It was not to be prepared for another relationship, but I wanted to make sure I wasn't mentally damaged by the things I was leaving behind. There were things that were said and done that should have crippled my self-esteem or affected my outlook on marriage as a whole. There is nothing anyone can say or do to help you heal from a divorce, except for allowing God to solely heal the brokenness. I needed closure for myself in order for me to properly move on without looking back and wondering. After much prayer, God provided me with the closure I needed and the understanding in why things went the way they did.

I encourage you that there is definitely happiness after divorce. The difference is: do you want temporary happiness that will help you to get over your divorce for that moment, or do you want genuine happiness for yourself that will last for the generation of your life whether you are alone or with someone? If you are one who didn't get the chance to experience self-happiness prior to entering a committed relationship, I urge you to take the time now to find that within yourself. Whether you are single or in a relationship now, begin to date yourself and spend time getting to know you. I'm not saying you deprive yourself from the relationship you are in, but more of finding a balance of doing both because ultimately if you become a better you, it will also benefit your relationship.

Please don't misunderstand me. My divorce was not an easy process, especially because it was drawn out, but I learned so much about myself and marriage. I am constantly being asked if I would give love and marriage another try, and my answer has always been, "Yes!" Marriage is a beautiful thing. I enjoyed being a wife and taking care of my family. However, marriage is not meant for everyone, and if you force someone into something they are not ready for, that increases the chances of it failing. Nonetheless. I wanted to focus more on the positive aspect from what I experienced, and in doing so I have grown tremendously as a person, a mother, and one day a wife. It was the formatting of this exact workbook that helped me to transition from one chapter of my life, into another.

Do your work. Heal yourself completely so the new you will grow and attract those of the same caliber as yourself. Always remember there is purpose in your pain and that everything you go through has a reason behind it.

1. What is your current relationship status?

_____

_____

_____

_____

_____

_____

_____

_____

_____

2. Are you happy/satisfied with that status? If not, why?

_____

_____

_____

_____

_____

_____

_____

_____

_____

_____

3. The situation you are in now, are you in by your own choosing or by someone else choosing for you? (No one can live your life better that you can, so stop letting everyone make suggestions for your life.).

_____

_____

_____

_____

_____

_____

_____

_____

_____

_____

4. Have you consulted God about your current relationship? (He is the only one that will be there through the good and the bad).

_____

_____

_____

Printed in the United States
By Bookmasters